Old and new Milwaukee Road locomotives assume a symbolic pose at the Milwaukee depot in July, 1951. The old and weary streamlined Pacific, which has brought the *Chippewa* from Chicago, is just about to move out of the way so the Erie-built FM unit can couple on the train to continue its journey into upper Michigan.

COVER ONE: Twin Cities-bound *Hiawatha* steams along the Mississippi River north of Winona, Minnesota.

COVER THREE: Eastbound Milwaukee Road *Hiawatha* speeds through Wisconsin Dells on an autumn day in 1937.

COVER FOUR: Chicago & NorthWestern *Minnesota 400* stops briefly at Winona, Minnesota on her regular run.

Chicago & NorthWestern-Milwaukee Road Pictorial

By Russ Porter

The C&NW *Viking* crack passenger train from Chicago to the Twin Cities stops at Ablemans, Wisconsin around 1950. The town's name was later changed to Rock Springs, and the depot was moved to the Mid-Continent Railway Museum at North Freedom.

1

Train No. 21, the *Chippewa,* lets off steam at the west end of the Milwaukee depot in 1937. Pacific No. 197 was one of a series of old locomotives modernized for *Chippewa* service.

DEDICATION

To the memory of my dad, Robert, who took me on so many of those train-chasing trips and also to the memory of longtime friend Bob Ferge, who accompanied me on many railroad photography excursions.

Library of Congress
Catalog Card Number: 94-75627

ISBN: 0-911581-30-8

Heimburger House Publishing Company
7236 West Madison Street
Forest Park, Illinois 60130

Printed in Hong Kong

2

Contents

Introduction

As a very young boy growing up in the Austin area of Chicago, I became acquainted with the Milwaukee Road. There was about a two-acre square lot between our house and the Milwaukee train yard. When my young cronies and I became tired of building and defending mud forts (World War I heroes were still fresh in our minds), we would go over to the railroad yard.

Sitting there was a long row of steam locomotives waiting to be scrapped. We spent many a happy hour sitting in the cabs and making believe we were engineers. Some of the locomotives still had balloon stacks, and at our young age, we figured it was possible some of them had been in early buffalo hunts.

We had many friends living in Lombard and Arlington Heights, two Chicago suburbs, so on weekends dad cranked up the Model T and off we'd go. The C&NW served both towns, so I managed to spend some time at the depots, watching freight and passenger trains. It was then I started to make pencil sketches of trains. I was becoming fascinated with trains and was already learning how to draw them.

We moved to Elmwood Park, another suburb of Chicago, in the early 1930s. From there I could ride a Milwaukee train to and from downtown Chicago. I still remember seeing the brand-new 1935

This is a 1990 view of the newly constructed Wisconsin Dells Milwaukee Road station, dedicated on June 10, 1989.

Milwaukee Road *Pioneer Limited* rushes past Kilbourn (now Wisconsin Dells) depot in this circa 1930 winter scene. The depot was destroyed in a 1986 coal train wreck.

steam-powered *Hiawatha* passenger train with its beautiful cars, including that very unusual beaver tail observation. I saw the train on a Saturday at Union Station, and I'll never forget it!

On another weekend, dad and I drove our 1934 Dodge along a road that followed the Milwaukee for some miles. Near Lake Forest we parked along with many other cars and waited for the *Hiawatha.* Sure enough, right on the advertised, we heard an air horn in the distance and within minutes, the train, swift as an arrow, sped by with the rear of the train obscured in a cloud of dust.

In 1940 I rode the *Hiawatha* to Milwaukee just to take photos of it on the curve at the west end of the depot. Also, in those early years, my dad rented a cottage at Devils Lake, Wisconsin. The cottage near the east bluff faced the C&NW tracks; I remember hearing the whistle of a train vibrating off the bluffs, as it came closer and closer. During the night, a passenger-mail train came through, waking everyone.

Yes, both railroads—the Milwaukee Road and the Chicago & NorthWestern—had a great influence on my life, not only as an everyday occurence, but also in forming an accurate visual aid in the preparation of railroad paintings which I do. The two railroad lines were and still are an inspiration to this railroad artist.

Russ Porter
West Allis, Wisconsin

5

Chicago & NorthWestern

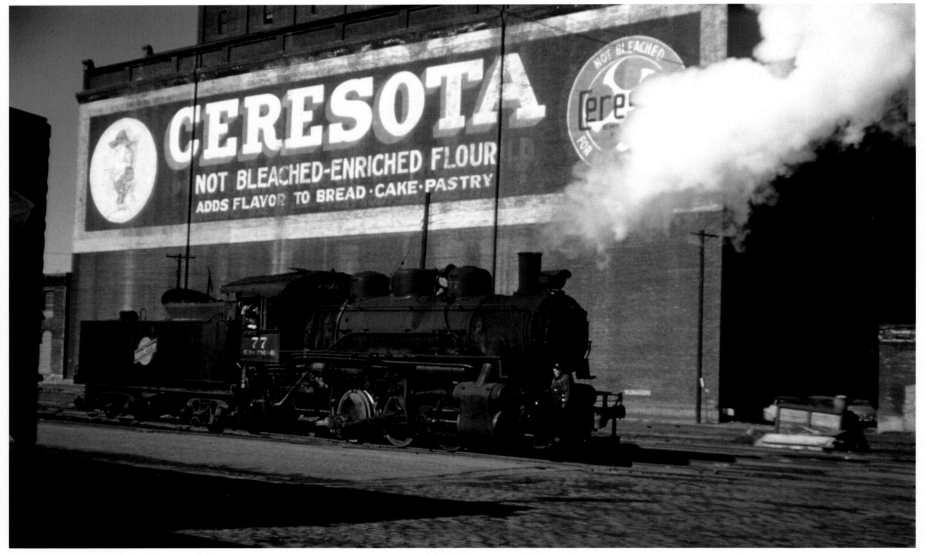

Many of these little capable 0-6-0 work horses were found scattered over the many yards and terminals of the giant C&NW. Here Class M-3 No. 77 switcher services the Ceresota flour mill at St. Paul, Minnesota in 1952.

ABOVE. The morning sun highlights the boiler fronts of a C&NW R1 4-6-0 and two M1 0-6-0 switchers near the C&NW yard office at Adams, Wisconsin in 1951. These engines will be at work soon. ABOVE, RIGHT. Grandma and grandson watch in 1954 as the westbound C&NW *Viking,* powered with an ex-"400" Pacific-type E2 locomotive, prepares to leave the Baraboo, Wisconsin, depot. After many more local stops, the *Viking* will reach the end of the journey at Minneapolis. RIGHT. In July of 1957, C&NW light Pacific-type E, No. 511, pulls its dark green commuter consist out of the Chicago coach yard on a hot, humid day (note the water level sweat mark on the tender side). Minutes later, the train backed into the C&NW depot, ready to accept the rush of home-bound passengers.

Heeding the hand signal of the brakeman, the engineer of this Alco S4 switcher No. 1093 gently pushes a cut of cars into the hold of the C&O car ferry *Spartan,* in the summer of 1955. Automobiles on the right will also go on board. On Oct. 3, 1980 railroad car ferry operation at Milwaukee, Wisconsin ceased.

Built for the C&NW in 1950, Budd cars journey into Chicago from Milwaukee past Class E Pacific No. 542 (right) soon to be scrapped. Later that year, the Budd cars, among the first 20 built, were traded to the C&O for three Pullman-built, lightweight coaches.

ABOVE. C&NW GP-7 No. 1589 sporting the "400" emblem on her sides, drifts downgrade at West Allis, Wisconsin in 1958. A local freight, the train is headed for Mitchell Yard, a few miles east. There it will set off and pick up cars for industries around Milwaukee. RIGHT. The last active steam locomotive in the Milwaukee area, C&NW Consolidation 2-8-0 No. 1899 rests forlornly in the Chase Avenue roundhouse in the Beer City. Her job in December of 1959 was to heat the roundhouse. Today a shopping center occupies the site.

After the Rain—1913. A summer shower ended, passengers alight from a westbound local at Clintonville, Wisconsin; the Class A Atlantic simmers quietly as the engineer and a passenger discuss the merits of the large drivers.

As the fireman on SD-9 No. 1707 watches, National Railway Historical Society members make their way back to the train after viewing the beauty of Devil's Lake, Wisconsin. The beautiful fall colors of the bluffs make a pleasing contrast with the yellow of the C&NW "400" cars of this special October, 1960 train.

A pair of SD-40-2's power a C&NW southbound freight, about to cross Potter Road in Wauwatosa. From the looks of the pilot on No. 6851, some heavy drifts had been encountered earlier. The bridge in the background is over the Milwaukee Road main line.

RIGHT. A week after this photo was taken in December of 1959, No. 1899 blew up, killing the night maintenance man. It was believed he fell asleep while sitting in the cab. Waking up and noticing the water level had dropped out of sight in the gauge, he quickly opened the water inlet valve. Unfortunately, the water had been gone for a long time, and when the cold water hit the hot, dry crown sheet, the boiler blew. See page 10.

LEFT. In December of 1963 heavy white vapors from a leaking steam pipe spiral upward from between a passenger and mail car on C&NW train No. 149. It's a very cold day at the Milwaukee lakefront depot as No. 149 prepares to depart for Green Bay. BELOW. Train No. 206, *Green Bay "400"* from Green Bay, passes Grand Avenue Tower in 1967 enroute to the new Milwaukee Road depot in Milwaukee, having come onto Milwaukee tracks at Canco Junction on the "Beer Line" tracks behind the "400" and the Milwaukee main line west, shown curving to the left.

THE attractive special-ties shown herein are offered at popular prices in the form of Club Service. ℂ Under this arrangement patrons will be served a lesser portion than that which would be furnished from the regular a la carte menu.

CHICAGO & NORTH WESTERN RY.

DINING CAR SERVICE

SERVED TO ONE PERSON ONLY

DINNER
NUMBER ONE

BROILED WHITEFISH
FRENCH FRIED POTATOES
GREEN PEAS

45 CENTS

PLEASE ORDER BY NUMBER ONLY

BREAD AND BUTTER 10 CENTS
COFFEE, PER CUP, 10 CENTS
MILK, PER GLASS, 10 CENTS

C&NW #503 prepares to leave the stub end depot in LaCrosse, Wisconsin. Powered by a venerable Class D Atlantic, the train from Chicago eventually will end its journey in Pierre, South Dakota.

On a C&NW spur in June of 1965 a switcher cautiously pokes its nose out from behind an old street car barn at 84th and Becher streets in West Allis, Wisconsin. Today the barn has been replaced by a shopping mall, and the trolley bus is, of course, gone.

Train No. 121, *Streamliner 400* destined for Green Bay, waits on this rainy night as a brakeman, flashlight shining, checks the car journals. Passengers are already on board, and soon the C&NW depot will vibrate with the sound of the diesel's engines coming to life.

In August of 1941, C&NW Class H Northern-type 4-8-4 No. 3031 heads for the Omaha stockyards with a string of empty cars. Locomotive No. 3031 was built by Baldwin in 1929. Before diesels appeared, this Class H locomotive powered the Chicago-San Francisco *Overland Limited*. It was scrapped in 1955.

After leaving the new Milwaukee depot, bi-level streamliner No. 121 swings north off the Milwaukee main line at Grand Avenue Junction. In just a little over a year from February, 1970, this train will cease to exist, thus bringing an era of famed "400" trains to Green Bay to an end.

C&NW southbound *Peninsula 400* makes an impressive sight in May of 1965 as it crosses the long bridge at Manitowoc. This deluxe train with the latest bi-level equipment consisted of a dining car, tap lounge, coach-bar-lounge, parlor car and coaches.

Milwaukee-bound shoppers in 1967 converse as the C&NW southbound *Peninsula 400* prepares to stop at Port Washington, Wisconsin, the last stop before Milwaukee.

Escanaba, Michigan was for years a mecca for C&NW FM baby Train Masters. Here in September, 1968 are three FM H16-66's awaiting assignment to the ore yard where they will pick up cars loaded with iron ore pellets from the mine at Ishpeming. The coaling tower in the background is a symbol of another time when steam reigned. The date is September, 1968.

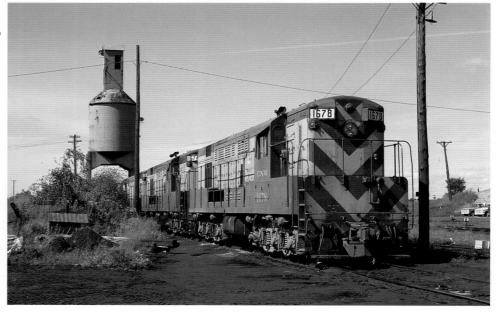

A southbound C&NW pulpwood train approaches Powers, Michigan depot in October, 1969. The lead unit, FM class H16-66 baby Train Master No. 1906, had the distinction of being the last of her class built for the C&NW in 1956. While the appearance of the depot belies it, Powers is an important railroad junction—tracks radiate to Escanaba and Menominee, Michigan and to Ashland, Wisconsin.

There's plenty of activity in this August, 1970 scene. C&NW FM Class H10-44 switcher No. 97 gets ready to shove a pair of hoppers aboard the Chesapeake & Ohio car ferry *City of Midland* No. 41. At the right, automobiles get ready to be driven to the top deck of the ferry. In five hours crossing Lake Michigan the ferry will deposit its cargo at Ludington.

Holiday passengers discharged, #1097 is ready to depart Wilton, Wisconsin on the Elroy-Sparta line.

With the head brakeman riding the front step, ready to flip the turnouts, Alco No. 1213 Class S-1 belches black smoke as it moves out of a Oconto, Wisconsin siding. These cars of pulpwood will soon be coupled onto the main line cars. Peshtigo, Wisconsin is the next town of work for this busy local train.

A Janesville to Fond du Lac C&NW freight waits for a westbound Milwaukee Road freight to clear the diamond at Watertown, Wisconsin in July of 1971. Some years later, with business falling off, the C&NW track was torn up and the diamond removed. In the mid-80s with coal traffic booming, the track and diamond were restored.

In weather an Eskimo would enjoy, a C&NW freight, led by Alco No. 1026 Class RS-1 blurs through a highway crossing on the northern outskirts of Mason City, Iowa in April, 1971. Only a few hours later all highways leading into the city were closed.

22

With brake shoes smoking, an empty coal train comes down the long grade, past the West Allis depot. Locomotive No. 1682, an FM product, Class H16-66 junior Train Master, leads the way in April of 1973.

ABOVE. C&NW commuter train #711 comes to the end of the line at Lake Geneva, Wisconsin in August of 1973. Locomotive #505 is a "Crandall Cab" unit, converted from an E-9B and named for its designer. Eleven ex-Union Pacific E-9b's were converted for Chicago suburban service in the early part of 1973. ABOVE, RIGHT. Late at night the C&NW enginehouse at Butler, Wisconsin is a quiet place. When morning comes, maintenance work will begin on EMD No. 1219 Class SW-1200 and FM No. 1677 Class H16-66 junior Train Master. RIGHT. With lead unit EMD No. 831 Class GP-35 rounding the curve, a freight from Madison heads for Wyeville, Wisconsin. Here at Ablemans the picturesque bluffs are gradually being reduced by the railroad quarrying of rock for ballast along its track.

On a sunny but cold morning, and with fresh snow making a picture-perfect scene, two freights pass on the main line between Mitchell Yard and St. Francis, Wisconsin. Long ago the railroad wisely depressed the track in this area, thus eliminating many grade crossings and increasing train speed.

Due to the collapse of its tunnel at Tunnel City, Wisconsin, the C&NW obtained trackage rights on the Milwaukee Road. Thus, C&NW freight with EMD GP-35 No. 821 leading, emerges in April of 1976 from the west portal of the Milwaukee Road tunnel and leans into the curve towards Sparta. The sight of a caboose sandwiched between the diesel is unusual. Just above the leading diesel is the partially hidden portal of the original tunnel; seeping water caused its abandonment. To the left, beyond the high mound and not in sight, is the C&NW abandoned tunnel.

It's a very cold March, 1976
day as EMD No. 976 Class
SD-45 leads a freight eastbound near Lebanon, Wis-
consin, stirring up a cloud
of snow. The fast freight is
enroute from the Twin
Cities to Milwaukee.

A track removal train is
at the C&NW depot in
Sparta, Wisconsin in
1976. The roadbed from
Sparta to Elroy has
become a well-known
bicycle trail with three
tunnels for added inter-
est. The Sparta depot is
now the bicycle trail
headquarters at the
west end of the trail.

27

Night operator at Jefferson Jct., Wisconsin hands up orders to fireman on a Madison-bound train.

LEFT. Eastbound freight works hard on the grade out of Butler, Wisconsin. Destination: Sheboygan and Green Bay. Lead unit is EMD No. 6808 Class SD-40-2, and the trailing unit is Alco No. 6703 Class C628, formerly of the Norfolk & Western.

BELOW, LEFT. Bessemer & Lake Erie No. 839 pays a visit to the C&NW terminal in 1978 at Butler, Wisconsin. C&NW EMD No. 6846 Class SD-40-2 stands on the next track while EMD No. 417 F-7 looms large in the camera lens.

BELOW, RIGHT. A scene from the past! Mid-Continent Railway Museum's C&NW No. 1385 ten-wheeler powers a business car special through the Soo Line, ex-Milwaukee Road tunnel at Tunnel City, Wisconsin. The date of October, 1955 was the last time a steam locomotive had gone through the tunnel. Milwaukee Road Class S-2 No. 204 4-8-4 going eastbound with a freight, had that honor. Photo was taken in June of 1985.

With a friendly wave from the fireman, SD-40-2 No. 6860 rushes its cargo around a sweeping curve just east of Lebanon, Wisconsin. The terrain in this part of Wisconsin consists of small hills and gullies, thus necessitating the track to wind in and out, up and down.

ABOVE. With the turnout set, a brakeman prepares to board C&NW switcher No. 1041. It is a rainy October day in 1963 at Sterling, Illinois, and ex-GTW steam switcher 0-6-0 works with cars for the nearby Northwestern Steel and Wire Company. LEFT. A recent derailment in 1963 at this turnout makes the crew cautious as GP-7 switcher No. 1645 moves slowly forward. Jones Island, Milwaukee is a busy shipping port, so the track crew is always on call.

31

ABOVE, LEFT. Proudly displaying the C&NW emblem on its nose, the "Eden Turn" local freight scampers eastbound from Butler, Wisconsin. Evidently the front emblem was just a passing thought, as the railroad never applied it to its other power with the exception of the F units. ABOVE. C&NW eastbound freight with SD-40-2 No. 6810 leading, comes down grade on the first day of 1976 at West Allis in a New Year's day blizzard. The street crossing has already been blocked by a stalled westbound train which will soon have the help of a pusher locomotive from Mitchell Yard. LEFT. Westbound freight with SD-40-2's Nos. 6892 and 6894 pulls out of the Mississippi river front yard at St. Paul, in August, 1986. Minutes later the train will cross the river and head for Minneapolis and towns west.

The Milwaukee Road

Baltic No. 135, on standby service in 1941, awaits assignment at the Milwaukee Road depot in Milwaukee. Earlier, on July 20, 1934, a similar Baltic No. 6402 reached a speed of 103.5 mph during a special test run between Chicago and Milwaukee.

PREVIOUS PAGE. At Janesville in May, 1950, Milwaukee- Road Baltic No. 133 is the headend power for the Chicago-bound *Varsity,* which began her trip at Madison, Wisconsin. On the track nearest the depot, Ten-Wheeler No. 1105 is ready to depart for Mineral Point.

RIGHT. Seen from the doorway of the wheel shop building, a 1950 westbound *Morning Hiawatha* is a colorful sight. The train is just about to go under the interurban line bridge and head for Grand Avenue Junction where the Milwaukee Road divides to the west and north.

LEFT. Milwaukee Road's Train No. 25, the *Southwest Limited* to Kansas City, passes over the flooding Fox River, approaching the tower at the Soo crossing at Burlington, Wisconsin about 6 p.m. on April 29, 1951. Today, the train, track and the tower is gone, and the Soo Line trackage is now the Wisconsin Central.

35

LEFT. Locomotive Class S-2 4-8-4 No. 220 steams southward from Milwaukee on a below zero morning in January of 1954. The locomotive is beginning to hit its stride after cresting the long hill at Lake Tower. ABOVE. Looking the worse for wear, the original 1935 *Hiawatha* No. 1, now degraded to a secondary train, races through Sturtevant, Wisconsin. The grand old legend can still kick up dust on the people on the platform.

Faced with mechanical problems, the crew of a 1951 northbound *Hiawatha* gets ready to bring out the detractable coupler for a tow into Milwaukee. This became unnecessary as a four-unit freight came up behind, uncoupled from its train and pushed the passenger train to Milwaukee.

Westbound way freight moves majestically toward a country road, just north of Elm Grove, Wisconsin in January, 1952. With the temperature at 20 below zero and a cold, strong wind blowing, this photograph was taken through the windshield of the car.

In March of 1951 southbound Class S-2 4-8-4 No. 231 moves rapidly with plumes of smoke and steam trailing. The air is cold and crisp outside, but the engine crew is warm in the spacious all-weather cab.

Meeting of the Tribe—Two *Hiawathas* meet a third at New Lisbon, Wisconsin.

With the heavy smoke billowing from its stack, Ten-Wheeler No. 1038, with a streamlined combine trailing, leaves Janesville in May of 1954 to pick up freight cars in the nearby yard. Afterward, it will head for Mineral Point, working towns along the way. The combine, built to resemble the 1935 *Hiawatha* cars, was equipped with kerosene lights.

A mixed train from Janesville arrives at Gratiot, Wisconsin in May of 1954 enroute to Mineral Point. On this side of the depot, the track once went to Schullsburg, a lead mining town much like Mineral Point. It's hard to believe that 12 passenger trains passed through here daily in the 1900's.

BELOW. National Railway Historical Society members stretch their legs in Madison, Wisconsin during an excursion run in May, 1954. Milwaukee Road Pacific No. 171 with its string of *Hiawatha* cars has the appearance of one of the *Chippewa* trains. Locomotive No. 171 was scrapped right after this trip.

ABOVE. With the signal giving the green "go ahead," S-2 4-8-4 No. 204 shakes the ground as it thunders across the North Avenue crossing near Elm Grove, Wisconsin. This was the last time (October, 1955) this locomotive passed here; next, the scrap yard. RIGHT. The last Milwaukee Road steam locomotive operating into Milwaukee waits for a signal near Elm Grove. The No. 204, though showing signs of neglect, still has the massive look of power that these big Northerns were noted for. Asked about the green flags flying on the boiler front, the engineer said that there was another diesel-powered section following.

Milwaukee Road Erie-built diesel FM unit powering a passenger train at high speed, nears the Elgin, Joliet & Eastern crossing at Rondout, Illinois. The train is enroute from Chicago to Milwaukee in May of 1961. When new the FM diesel helped power the *Olympian* to and from the West Coast.

LEFT. The tender of S-3 4-8-4 No. 265 reflects the image that spelled doom for steam power. Luckily, this tender and its locomotive is now safe from the scrapper's torch, resting at the Illinois Railway Museum in Union. The photo was taken in Milwaukee in November, 1955.

BELOW. 1,000 hp diesel No. 5901 comes east into Wauwatosa, Wisconsin at the head end of the commuter train *Cannonball*. This unit, like its twin, was built at the railroad's Milwaukee shops in 1958. Both units were used in Montana and ended their days on runs in Wisconsin.

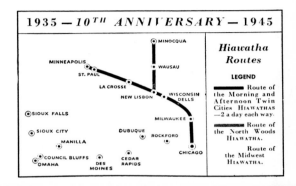

1935 — 10ᵀᴴ ANNIVERSARY — 1945

Hiawatha Routes

LEGEND

Route of the Morning and Afternoon Twin Cities HIAWATHAS —2 a day each way.

Route of the North Woods HIAWATHA.

Route of the Midwest HIAWATHA.

Locomotive S-3 4-8-4 No. 265 sits idle in Milwaukee in November of 1955. In 1956 it was given to the City of Milwaukee by the railroad and put in a park near Lake Michigan on the southeast side of the city. On March 27, 1975 the locomotive was moved to the Illinois Railway Museum at Union.

FM "C-Liners," with No. 23C leading, bring a 1961 southbound freight to the top of the grade at Lake Tower, located about seven miles from downtown Milwaukee.

ABOVE, LEFT. FM Class H12-44 No. 702 with a sister awaits a cut of cars at the Air Line yard hump office in Milwaukee. The yard had a capacity of 1,087 cars in its 24 track area. It was the first in railroad history to combine automatic switching and retarder speed control.

ABOVE, RIGHT. Twin Cities-bound *Afternoon Hiawatha* rounds a curve in March of 1965 about two miles north of Wisconsin Dells. Down the embankment, to the right of the sky top observation car, can be seen the snow-covered 15 inch gauge track of the little steam-powered Riverside & Great Northern Railway.

LEFT. Duplex-roomette sleeping car *Gallatin River* waits in September of 1964 for the arrival from Chicago of the *Pioneer Limited*. The time is 11:30 p.m., and the sleeper passengers are either bedded down or await the gentle coupling jolt as the car is added to the *Limited*. At 11:40 p.m. the train will depart from the old Milwaukee depot and head for the Twin Cities.

A Milwaukee Road passenger train destined for Chicago, headed by EMD FP-7A No. 104C, readies for a November, 1965 departure from Milwaukee. The new depot is bathed in light; soon the new post office building will shut out this view of the depot and other buildings, creating a tunnel-like appearance of these tracks. No. 104C was eventually moved to the Illinois Railway Museum.

NEXT PAGE. Eastbound 1937 *Hiawatha* emerges from portal at Tunnel City, Wisconsin on Christmas Eve day.

ABOVE. As the towerman waves a greeting, the eastbound *Morning Hiawatha,* racing at 70 miles per hour, is about to clatter over the Soo Line diamond at Duplainville, Wisconsin. After checking the rest of the train for possible hot journals, the towerman climbs the stairs to the welcome warmth of the tower on this Christmas Day in 1968.

RIGHT. Westbound freight pulls slowly out of the Savanna, Illinois yard under the watchful eye of the towerman. The smoking F units, trailed by a switcher, are just about to cross the CB&Q Chicago-Twin Cities main line.

50

A Milwaukee Road switchman chats with the crew of freshly painted EMD F-7 No. 47C. On a nearby track, the fireman is busy attending the innards of FM H12-44 No. 749 switcher, as it waits for the westbound main line train to clear the track at "Cut-off Tower" in Milwaukee.

A few miles from Portage, Wisconsin a quartet of EMD F-7's, with No. 79A in the lead, prepares to go beneath a country road bridge at Lewiston. Due to financial difficulties in 1968, the weed-covered tracks show poor maintenance, thus the train's speed is reduced considerably.

EMD GP-40 No. 2033 leads a southbound empty ore train around a curve over freshly ballasted main line track on the outskirts of Milwaukee. The long train has just descended Lake Hill and begins to hit its stride for a short time before arriving at Milwaukee in March of 1974.

In November of 1971, the last of five such units, EMD FP-45 No. 5, with stacks smoking heavily, blasts past the Wisconsin Dells depot. The northbound train is just about to cross the bridge over the Wisconsin River and the highway leading into that tourist town.

EMD GP-40 No. 2071 heads an August, 1972 northbound freight on the wrong main, two miles north of Wisconsin Dells. No. 2071 was the last GP-40 furnished to the Milwaukee Road and was leased before being purchased.

The Milwaukee Road depot in Milwaukee still retained its classic tower when the eastbound *Morning Hiawatha* made its daily stop in July of 1951. Passengers are disembarking and soon the distinctive parlor-observation car will follow its train around the curve and head for Chicago.

A busy place is Rondout, Illinois where the Milwaukee Road's north and south main lines cross the Elgin, Joliet & Eastern belt line. A southbound freight with EMD FP-7 No. 101A leading has just crossed the diamond and is about to block the tower in this 1973 view.

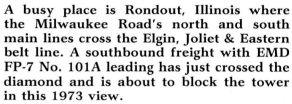

North Avenue crossing in Elm Grove, Wisconsin has always been a good location for photographing trains, and this May, 1972 morning is no exception. Running on the wrong main, the westbound freight, with EMD F-7 No. 110C on the point, is pouring out the smoke as it comes up grade.

56

A southbound freight with GP-40 No. 2027 leading, passes the well-maintained Milwaukee Road depot at Sturtevant, Wisconsin in November of 1972. Between the depot and No. 2027, a wye track branches west to a small yard and the line to Savanna, Illinois. The turnout leading toward the photographer goes to a small yard and a track which branched off the turnout and headed east to Racine.

Eastbound Milwaukee Road-Union Pacific domeliner *City of San Francisco* has just crossed the Mississippi River and the CB&Q Twin Cities main line and is now stopping briefly at the Milwaukee Road Savanna, Illinois depot. It's a very cold December 1967 day, and the maintenance men in the Chicago yard will have much work to do, as indicated by the leaking steam lines of the cars.

Five brand-new EMD MP-15 AC 1,500 hp units take a southbound train across KK bridge in Milwaukee. Time on the huge Allen-Bradley Company clock is 2:22 p.m. and the date is December 29, 1975. The bridge at left is the Chicago & NorthWestern entrance into downtown Milwaukee.

In March of 1972 GP-30 No. 1006 from Savanna, Illinois slowly rounds the north-bound wye track with a long freight bound for Milwaukee. The deteriorating shelter on the left once protected Sturte-vant passengers for the *Southwest Limited*.

NEXT PAGE. Nicknamed *The Ford Special* because of the cargo of automobiles it carries, SD-40-2 3,000 hp No. 139 leads a trio of units around a curve at Columbus, Wisconsin. It is westbound enroute to the Twin Cities in July of 1976.

TWIN CITIES Hiawathas

Baggage has been put aboard, the porters are ready to put the footsteps up, and the con-ductor is about ready to give the "All Aboard" signal. Within minutes, the *Morning Hiawatha* will silently glide away from the onlookers at the Portage depot, gaining momentum for the long trip to the Twin Cities. The date is September, 1968.

This 1976 westbound Milwaukee freight slowly approaches the east portal at Tunnel City, Wisconsin. Due to the collapse of the parallel tunnel on the Chicago & NorthWestern, trackage rights were arranged. The turnout, visible under the two lead units is part of the Chicago & NorthWestern track.

Westbound Milwaukee F units with No. 79C leading trail smoke as they emerge from the west portal at Tunnel City. The original tunnel opening is at upper right; water problems forced relocation of the bore.

At Camp Douglas, Wisconsin, eastbound Milwaukee coal train with GE U30C No. 5655 on the point speeds under abandoned Chicago & NorthWestern Sparta-Wyeville, Wisconsin line. A tunnel collapse caused the end of this line.

BELOW. Traffic on the nearby expressway was bogged down in both directions, but the ice and snow storm did not seem to bother this northbound Milwaukee freight with FP-45 No. 4 in the lead. I even received a friendly wave from the fireman, who probably was thinking, "What is this guy on snowshoes doing out in weather like this?"

Winding through the curves of Air Line Yard, an eastbound Milwaukee freight powered with F units is just about to set out and pick up some cars. It has come in from the Twin Cities and will terminate in Bensenville, Illinois.

63

With January storm clouds disappearing over Lake Michigan, the sun has come out brilliantly over downtown Milwaukee and is highlighting the side of a westbound freight. With SD-45 No. 10 leading and FP-45 No. 4 trailing, the train is moving slowly, preparing to change crews about a mile ahead at Cut-off Tower. Then it will head for the Twin Cities.

This is a busy place, with one freight in the siding, and a southbound freight powered with F units and loaded with automobile frames destined for Detroit on another track. On the northbound track to Milwaukee, a Turboliner is moving fast toward that city. The Lake Tower operator is busy this cold February morning in 1976.

From the County Highway 146 bridge west of Fall River, Wisconsin, a 1980 Milwaukee Road freight with GP-40 No. 2017 in front, is a magnificent sight to behold as it rounds a sweeping curve and heads toward Portage.

Southbound July, 1976 freight climbs the grade toward Lake Tower, and the old F units with No. 125 preceding, are working their utmost.

Just-new southbound Milwaukee 1935 *Hiawatha* races through Sturtevant, Wisconsin; Indian emblem was added to tender later.

LEFT. Chicago-bound Turboliner crosses to the southbound track at Rondout on a snowy February morning. In spite of the weather, the train's rear red markers glow brightly. GP-9 No. 304 gets ready to switch cars on the interchange track with the Elgin, Joliet & Eastern.

Downtown Wauwatosa has always been a good place to see Milwaukee Road action, and today is no exception. Here a westbound freight with SD-40-2's Nos. 135 & 131 as power, comes through the bridge at moderate speed. The fireman leisurely enjoys the scenery.

LEFT. Southbound local Milwaukee freight with F-9 No. 126A backs into a siding to pick up cars at Caledonia, 26 miles south of Milwaukee in December of 1972. Brakeman keeps a careful eye on the standing cars in this backup move.

Chicago, Milwaukee, St. Paul and Pacific Railroad Company

Five F units round a curve at Hoyt Park, Wisconsin. The westbound freight has its work cut out as the terrain is full of curves.

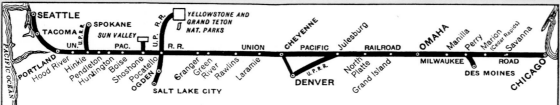

Fall colors are brilliant as an eastbound freight comes across the Soo Line diamond at Duplainville. The SD-40-2 sports good old number 202, once used on the railroad's Class S-2 4-8-4 steam locomotives. Hard to believe, but the freshly painted tower has also met the same fate as the steamer.

RIGHT. An eastbound freight leans into a long, sweeping curve at Lewiston, Wisconsin. The track was recently serviced, so the train is losing no time on its way to Portage, five miles distant.

BELOW, RIGHT. A Milwaukee freight from Bensenville descends a steep grade into the industrial section of Milwaukee. It's on its way to Burnham Yard, where it will be pulled apart and classified for distribution to other cities.

BELOW. Switching chores finished, the brakeman climbs the ladder to the warmth of No. 126A's cab as it moves southward in December, 1972 across the highway at Caledonia.

A 1977 southbound auto rack train for Detroit moves slowly from downtown Milwaukee. With GP-38-2 No. 358 leading, one can believe that an all-out effort will be mustered by the six units to bring the heavy train to the crest of Lake Hill, not too many miles south.

Two FM H12-44 1,200 hp switchers, Nos. 767 and 768, steam away in the below-zero March, 1972 weather at the "Cut-off" yard in Milwaukee, while awaiting assignment. No smoke is showing from the caboose stack, so evidently the caboose is going to be taken to the idle track. In 1939, the Milwaukee introduced the first brand-new steel bay window cabooses with the distinctive ribbed sides. Caboose No. 02000 is from the 1946 series. Final production of the ribbed side caboose was in 1951.

Passing an eastbound freight, a westbound freight with a mixture of power, including a deadheading Baldwin S10 1,000 hp switcher No. 934, curves toward the Portage, Wisconsin yard. Because of walkie-talkies, the yard track indicator at the right is no longer used.

Locomotive Characteristics

TYPE OF LOCOMOTIVE	"Milwaukee" Type
LENGTH OF LOCOMOTIVE	51 ft.-3 in.
LENGTH OF TENDER	37 ft.-5 in.
LOADED WEIGHT, driving	140,000 lbs.
LOADED WEIGHT, engine	280,000 lbs.
LOADED WEIGHT, tender	247,500 lbs.
WHEEL BASE, driving	8 ft.-6 in.
WHEEL BASE, engine	37 ft.-7 in.
WHEEL BASE, engine and tender	78 ft.-10½ in.
DRIVING WHEEL DIAMETER	7 ft.
CYLINDERS, diameter and stroke	19 in. x 28 in.
BOILER PRESSURE	300 lbs.
BOILER, diameter	76$\frac{11}{16}$ in.
TUBES, number and diameter	160—2¼ in.
TUBES, number and diameter	43—5½ in.
TUBES, length	19 ft.-0 in.
HEATING SURFACE, tubes	1781 sq. ft.
HEATING SURFACE, flues	1170 sq. ft.
HEATING SURFACE, firebox	254 sq. ft.
HEATING SURFACE, syphon	40 sq. ft.
HEATING SURFACE, total	3245 sq. ft.
SUPERHEATING SURFACE	1029 sq. ft.
FIREBOX	132½ in. x 75$\frac{3}{16}$ in.
GRATE AREA	69 sq. ft.
TENDER CAPACITY, water	13,000 gals.
TENDER CAPACITY, fuel oil	4,000 gals.
MAXIMUM TRACTIVE POWER	30,700 lbs.

THESE floor plans graphically illustrate the roominess of the HIAWATHA. Reading from top to bottom, the cars are shown in order beginning with the rear end of the train. The four coaches are all identical with the one illustrated. Every car is brand new and exemplifies the last word in travel comfort.

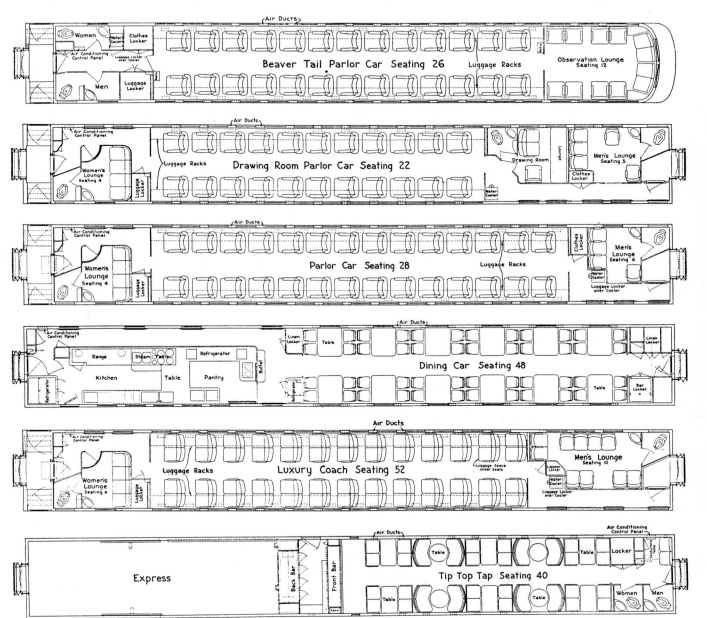

A Sunday morning in June of 1965 finds the Milwaukee Road engine terminal in Milwaukee quiet, with only a few units ready for assignment. A lone passenger unit in yellow paint separates the orange freight units. Evening will find many of these units active.